M000228440

PRAISE FOR
20 EFFECTIVE HABITS FOR MASTERY AT WORK

'Cindy Wahler gives us an easily comprehended roadmap for developing and practicing those personal behaviors at work that will deliver the multitude of rewards that flow from a winning workplace culture. Great executives and managers build great teams by building great cultures. Cindy tells us how these 20 individual behaviors become the essential building blocks of great workplace cultures'

Eric Markell,
Board Director at ENMAX Corporation

'Cindy captures the very essence of leadership, offering a practical, straightforward guide that provides a pathway for implementing essential skills in the workplace. This book is a must read for those aspiring to leadership as well as for leaders looking to enhance their effectiveness'

Neil Tabatznik,
Founder of Tshemba Foundation,
and Director at Blue Ice Group Company

'A motivating workplace culture is at the heart of every successful organization. It also requires relentless nurturing. What Cindy offers in 20 Effective Habits is a tangible, practical set of essential habits and insights leaders can turn to time and again to stay on the right track'

Jennifer Holmes Weier,
President & CEO at JA Central Ontario

'Cindy's insights on what makes a successful leader are always spot on. Invaluable strategies for those who want to improve their effectiveness'

Michael Duschenes,
Managing Director at Perimeter Institute

'Today's business world demands not just business skills and industry knowledge, it requires a mastery of the self. The best leaders carve out time to cultivate self-awareness, emotional intelligence, and a critical suite of "soft" social skills. This book is an excellent companion on this lifelong journey'

Claire Cockerton,
Managing Director at Cockerton & Co,
and Co-Founder of Innovate Finance,
Level39, Plexal, and ENTIQ

'Dr Cindy Wahler's 20 Habits lay out a clear action plan for behavioural change to drive workplace success, informed by deep experience of coaching senior leaders to higher levels of performance for themselves and their organizations. Cindy's wisdom and engaging communication style ensure that the reader will take away practical and actionable lessons that can be put into effect in any setting'

Phillip Doyle, CFA,
Vice President at Burgundy Asset Management Ltd

20 EFFECTIVE HABITS FOR MASTERY AT WORK

By **Cindy Wahler**

Editor: Derin Cag

20 Effective Habits for Mastery at Work

To my husband Leon, son Josh, and dog Ranger,

The three most special men in my life.

CONTENTS

ABOUT THE AUTHOR

Cindy Wahler, PhD, is a leadership consultant with broad based experience in positioning organisations for success within both the private and public sectors. She places an emphasis on developing next generation leaders as well as seasoned senior executives. She has worked for a wide variety of Fortune 100 and Fortune 500 companies representing a cross-section of industry sectors.

Sample clients include AstraZeneca, British Telecom, Columbia University, Deutsche Post DHL, ENMAX, Exxon Mobil Corp, Hilti, The Home Depot, IMAX, KPMG, Mercer, Ontario Teachers Pension Plan, Ralph Lauren, Royal Bank of Canada, Sara Lee, Scotiabank, SickKids Foundation, Teva, Toronto Dominion Bank, Toyota, and Zurich Insurance - to name a few.

As a contributor, Cindy regularly writes on Forbes, Huffington Post, CNN, Richtopia, and CEO Magazine. She has also been a regular guest on a variety of podcasts. She can be heard on Spotify, Google Podcasts, Apple Podcasts, Spreaker, and Anchor FM. Some of her podcasts can also be seen on YouTube. She writes and speaks on a variety of leadership topics that include: Empowering Women, Attracting Top Talent, Leading Remote Teams, Imposter Syndrome, and Executive Presence.

Cindy earned a Doctorate in Clinical Psychology from the University of Ottawa. She is a Certified Organisational Psychologist with a Major in Leadership Development, Ontario College of Psychologists since 1987.

INTRODUCTION

We often get asked what it means to have mastery at work and how to have the greatest positive impact on those we lead. The answer differs according to where the organisation is relative to its business cycle and growth strategy. There are a set of core skills or leadership habits that are pertinent to success. Our objective is to take these leadership attributes from conceptual notions to actual behaviour based skills.

This book presents a unique offering from other business books on leadership by explicitly identifying which habits or skills you will need to succeed in your career. The good news is that these skills are all measurable and actionable. The premise for these habits is to start with focused attention and concerted practice. You can learn how to incorporate these habits into your lexicon of leadership skills over time.

The intent is to make these habits second nature and call upon them depending upon who you are leading. Understanding the heart and soul of the people you are working with is paramount, especially if you want to attract and work with the very best of talent. Individuals who feel heard, listened to, respected, and rewarded for their contribution will be motivated to work harder and exhibit greater engagement and pride in their work. These habits will allow you to create and grow your leadership style to effect positive change. You will be able to foster an environment reflective of diversity of thought and inclusion for your own professional development as well as the teams you lead.

There are times when people get to be in leadership positions, and they may not have the composite set of skills to oversee the health and well-being of their organisation and their employees. Although we may question these decisions, there may be many reasons why they were appointed and may remain in their role for a length of time. Perhaps they were the right leader at the right time; however, the world or the economy has changed, and their skillset may no longer be relevant. Or possibly, their sponsor has a blind spot and does not see how they may be contributing to retention risks or jeopardising the company's financial well-being. So for these individuals, we can hope they are open to feedback, have some degree of self-awareness and seek to develop more effective skills to garner credibility with their team or the board. If not, the best we can ask for is that these individuals save face, demonstrate humility, and pass the baton.

Outstanding leadership is about acquiring a toolkit of skills that you call upon depending upon the type of individuals and personalities you work with, teams you lead, and challenges you may face. Adapting to your peers, direct reports, and the competitive landscape is central. As a leader, when you can rely on a fluid communication style, then you demonstrate the ability to adapt to so many different scenarios. The goal of every business is not to make the most money; the goal is to stay in business forever. As these are learned behaviours and habits, you can acquire these skills and serve as a positive role model for others. You are a leader at every level from the start of your career to the rise of your success, whether as an employee or an entrepreneur. Let us show you how it's done.

Habit #1

. . . .

COLLABORATING

"Life is not what you alone make it. Life is the input of everyone who touched your life and every experience that entered it. We are all part of one another."

~ Yuri Kochiyama

No one gets anywhere completely by themselves. You may begin with a great idea or even better, a revolutionary idea. Here's the deal. Remember those kids in the sandbox who never shared their toys? Maybe growing up we revered these kids as they had the best and most shiny objects. Yet the wiser we became, the more we realised they were lone soldiers alienating themselves along the way. Their allure and sheen wore off.

I had a client who in high school was bullied and ridiculed. He was indeed smarter than most, however, he was never one of the hip kids. He shared his ideas for machine learning and was laughed at by his classmates. Today he is a multi-millionaire and a serial entrepreneur. These bullies called him once he had media coverage, appealing to his ego. Of course, he remembered vividly how they alienated him and recognised they would never be able to be team players. My client believed that despite any potential maturing, he was not sure their core values of camaraderie and teaming would define their character. It was clear they were interested in riding his coattails, and of course, he has enough self-respect to never let that happen.

At work, if you are not a team player, then you are seen as an idea hog. You are viewed as running your own race. Unless you are in an individual sport such as a sprinter, a downhill skier or a diver, an absence of collaboration will never get you there.

Think about what you want out of your career. Whether you aspire to be at the top of the house or whether you want to make a difference in your defined space, the bottom line is you need others. Surrounding yourself with other people stimulates your thinking and helps you better articulate your concepts.

Why you ask? It would help if you assumed that although you have a compelling idea, all ideas benefit from additional input. Shared perspectives allow for views to shift from good to great. Your peers have different backgrounds, training and areas of expertise, which allow your ideas or initiatives to blossom. The goal is to maximise your impact. We know that organisations that foster high performing teams are ones that value collaborative problem-solving.

Collaboration can turn a good idea into a great idea. By collaborating, team members can build upon each others' notions. No matter how creative or insightful you are, your concepts can always benefit from a different point of view or a fresh, new perspective. Collaborative thinking allows a team to take advantage of everybody's knowledge and experience. As individuals, we each have different strengths. Partnering on initiatives can draw upon each of these strengths. Furthermore, a team will always be more robust than a collection of individuals.

Secondly, you cannot single-handedly promote an idea all by yourself. Your team members also have clout and organisational currency. In other words, you need them to help sell your idea to both their own teams and the broader organisation. You may not have influence with certain decision-makers, but what is central is that some of your peers do and it is vital to leverage them. Top-down leadership is an outdated and failed style of leadership. The objective is that when you get others to weigh in, then the journey and eventual success is a shared outcome.

When you collaborate, you create a groundswell. There is momentum and most importantly shared ownership, with many people having skin in the game. It is the best way to increase your odds of being successful. Do it through others, and you will win. Do it yourself, and you are on a lonely journey fraught with insurmountable obstacles. Plus celebrating success is better with other people rather than by yourself.

Lionel Messi is perhaps the greatest soccer player of this generation though he has never won the World Cup. Conner McDavid is arguably the best hockey player of this generation, and he has never won the Stanley Cup. Being a superstar in a team sport doesn't bring success if the team surrounding that superstar does not perform. The same is true in the workplace. While it is great to have superstar performers, they cannot do everything all by themselves.

There is an old adage that "a chain is only as strong as its weakest link". Teams often rely on their superstars to do the heavy lifting and overlook the supporting team members. Workplace demands are constantly increasing, and competition is ever-present. Reliance on a super performer may result in too much pressure on one individual and insufficient accountability for others.

What happens if your top performer gets a better offer and leaves? Do you have the bench strength to continue progressing? We must ensure that succession and development programs are available for all team members to invest in all key players, not just the superstars.

Diversity of thought and inclusion promotes the best solutions. High performing teams and leaders who win and excel do so with the help of others. Collaboration is a must-have, not a nice to have.

The Flipside of Collaborating

Although collaboration is vital, there is a balance. Take input and adapt and adjust your data points or your perspective. Everybody has a vote, but not an equal vote. This imbalance means that you should listen to other views and then make the final call. Do not be like the PhD student that never graduates because they are forever collecting more data. Take in all the input and collect best practices and then go forward with conviction.

When taken too far, collaboration can be paralysing, and you run the risk of missing out on time and place. Even worse, your competitor may steal your thunder. How often do you hear from entrepreneurs or those who like to innovate, "I had that very idea!" Sadly, they moved too slowly.

The difference between unanimity and collaboration is significant. Unanimity means you look for 100 per cent of your team or your peers to be on board. Collaboration means most people are with you, and you go forward and lead your team forward. Some may choose not to be on the bus, which is okay because you have enough players inside the tent, fired up and ready to go.

ACTION STEPS FOR COLLABORATING

1. Openly share ideas.

2. Partner with people who are energised by collaborative problem-solving.

3. Admit vulnerability, acknowledge you don't have all the answers.

4. Prepare to challenge and be challenged.

Habit #2

. . . .

LEADING

"Leaders aren't born; they are made. And they are made just like anything else, through hard work. And that's the price we'll have to pay to achieve that goal, or any goal."

~ Vince Lombardi

E arly in our careers, the way to be successful is to promptly achieve our targets. Come in on time and budget, and you are golden. Then repeat. In other words, you cannot be a one-hit-wonder; you must show a consistent track record. A consistent track record demonstrates your credibility. It shows that it wasn't luck but rather due to your habits and your skillset. People then want to bet on you.

When you do this, good things happen. You are recognised and rewarded. It means you are likely to get promoted from an individual contributor role to a leader of people. You now have earned the privilege of leading more complex projects. These projects involve multiple variables and require resources to get things done. You also now have different personalities to both manage and lead. This responsibility can be daunting. Many leaders never receive training on leading others; they are overwhelmed and second-guess what it means to lead. Going from managing to leading in many ways is a quantum leap. Knowing how to get there is paramount. This is where you must shift from being in the weeds to leading others. This is the biggest lesson or shift a new people manager must make. If you don't, you put the project at risk and jeopardise a culture of empowerment.

No one likes a micromanager. We have all had them. They annoy us because they tell us what to do. They take away our self-esteem and erode our self-confidence. They create self-doubt and stymie our ideas and the ability to move things forward.

We need to differentiate between a task manager and a leader. A manager focuses on tasks while a leader focuses on people. A manager will tell people what to do while a leader will help facilitate the conversation, brainstorm with their direct reports. The beauty of this process is that your direct reports will conclude they came to the answer all by themselves. In a way they did, you as a leader provided the environment to foster their thinking and opened their mind to solutions. A manager will make sure that a task gets achieved while a leader will give people the chance to succeed.

Sometimes my clients tell me that they believe being a good boss means to roll up their sleeves and be in the trenches with their direct reports. They see this as a benevolent gesture. At the end of the day, they are not appreciated as they message a lack of trust. Additionally, valuable energy that should be preserved for more forward-thinking initiatives is now lost.

At the very core, successful leaders must have the ability to attract great talent. After all, your team are your first point of contact. They will be eager to be part of your mission only when they trust that you are honest, transparent and convey a set of principles and ethics guided by the commitment of open and caring communication. If you as a leader are guided exclusively by the bottom line, your team might eventually choose to work elsewhere. Disenfranchised people are less productive, take less pride in their work, make greater mistakes and speak poorly of their leaders. An environment that fosters a culture where people matter is vital to your effectiveness and success as a leader.

Your role as a people manager is to build a talent pipeline. By delegating tasks, you create an environment that encourages engagement and reinforces retention. One of your metrics is to develop a successor, be it for your role or a role within your broader organisation. A true leader does not look for credit, but instead, they seek to give credit. They create an environment where team members are inspired and want to follow their lead.

Your team feels motivated when they feel valued. Valued for their ideas and valued for their contribution. When this happens, they will work hard for you. Yes, maybe your team is not solving problems the way you do, and yes, perhaps their work is not your gold standard. What is critical to ask yourself is "When is good, good enough"?

This question also frees you up to rise to the next level of your contribution. When you pull out of the weeds, you can engage in broader thinking. You can then put your energy into contributing more strategically. This contribution allows your creative juices to flow where you solve for tomorrow and the longer-term solution. Your brand then shifts from a transactional leader to one that helps to future proof your business. Now you have greater currency. When you can do this, you have leveraged your team's talent, and you are viewed as a leader who is instrumental in building an internal pipeline. You then go on to even more significant achievements.

The Flipside of Leading

It helps if you have your eye on the ball. In other words, empowering others does not mean you absolve yourself of your need to have oversight. Your team requires you to monitor how they are tracking. Are they achieving their goals in an efficient and timely manner? What obstacles are they running into? Great coaches are relied upon to run interference. They have the expertise and leverage to help remove barriers and suggest alternate approaches when their team is stuck.

Make sure you do not take empowerment too far. If you do, you run the risk of being an absentee leader. Absent leaders are liabilities. They run the risk of not course correcting, fostering divisiveness and an inability to create a culture of one team. Teams depend on your guidance and also require you to be a tie-breaker.

Some decisions are complex, and if you do not weigh-in, then someone has to settle the score. You are required to make the call. That is your responsibility as a leader. You need to ensure you weigh-in to keep things running efficiently and encourage the team to move forward.

Some people overload with leading and start acting based on impulse. Leadership requires decisive action. This type of leading is different from being impulsive. It is about collecting vital information and then making a decision and sticking by your decision. If you waver, you will appear skittish, uncertain and create doubt in your team.

Here's an example: A CEO of a major pharmaceutical company has a style of making an impulsive decision to terminate his employees. After 24 - 48 hours, he would hire these employees back. What prompted this roller coaster was a feeling of doubt, maybe these were critical members of his organisation. The culture he inadvertently created was one of doubt and fear. They did not see their CEO as being a stand-up leader. They then doubted his strategic plan and felt they were on shifting soil.

I recall another client who ran a major insurance company saying that the day she stopped feeling bad for terminations would be the day she would take down her shingle. Leaders must, at times, make unpopular decisions based on what is best for the business. The need to act decisively, whether it be firing an employee or divesting parts of the company is central to instilling confidence in the right leadership.

ACTION STEPS FOR LEADING

1. Assign roles and responsibilities and step back.

2. Dialogue with your directs by providing a platform for discussion. Help them generate solutions by challenging their thinking instead of giving them the solution.

3. Reward them for taking the initiative, trying things out and being creative.

4. Showcase their talent by giving them more visibility.

Habit #3

....

PRIORITISING

"To change your life, you need to change your priorities."

~ Mark Twain

Harr ow do you stay on top of tasks and make good judgement calls? How common is it to be working on something only to have a superior, a peer or a client ask you to stop everything and focus on a new or different task? It is annoying and disruptive and at times confusing. Your inner thought is probably, "I thought you told me to do this first."

It is rare to be faced with a single task or objective in the workplace. If anything, most of us have all (if not more) than we can handle. Trying to multitask and do everything at once is a recipe for disaster. The surest way of being successful is appropriate prioritising. Several factors need to be taken into account when assigning priorities to a variety of tasks:

- Timelines and available resources for different tasks.

- Where does your task fit into the broader enterprise? Whether or not others are dependent on you completing your task.

- The relative importance of the various tasks that you are evaluating.

- Do you have sole or joint responsibility for the task?

Prioritisation allows for seemingly unmanageable responsibilities to be broken down into individual steps to be mastered separately — sort of like weight loss. Maybe you have to lose 40 pounds, doctor's orders. So that is overwhelming. Start with a small focus or maybe one pound a week. Then add some exercise such as walking around the block. Once you have mastered the small steps or a few preliminary steps, you can add more vigorous exercise or healthy dietary habits. These accomplishments provide you with a sense of mastery which then allows you to complete other tasks.

It is important to remember that prioritisation should not be cast in stone. Prioritisation should be a fluid process where priorities are re-evaluated and shifted as conditions in the workplace change. New priorities may arise. Shifting workplace demands may cause specific tasks to rise or fall concerning their importance. Shifting deadlines may move timelines up or down. Resources that were available yesterday may not be there tomorrow.

Being able to prioritise as well as to alter priorities increases your ability to be successful. Letting go and changing what is on your list is also freeing as it gives you the flexibility to make decisions regarding what may be necessary.

Do not agonise over what should have or could have been. That is wasted energy, and you cannot rewrite history. The act of reflecting on what was supposed to be actioned is not a constructive use of your time and will bring you down. Instead, mobilise yourself to the new order of the day.

Setting personal goals and prioritising will contribute to your ability to be efficient at work. I once had a client who worked all day and night. She was prone to sending emails at 3:00 or 4:00 in the morning. When it came time for a promotion, she was given a high rating however she was not seen as a candidate for the role. Her boss advised me that if she is working this long and in this manner, how on earth would she ever stay afloat for a more prominent role.

The message in this anecdote is that in addition to the importance of creating personal time her extensive hours backfired. In essence, she was viewed as not being planful nor organised. Her manager told her that she worked harder than he does, yet she was not efficient nor mindful of her team members' personal and family time.

In essence, you should look at your list of priorities as a fluid and moving ledger. If you anticipate change, you will be able to adapt. Shifting gears requires cognitive flexibility - to recognise that you are never in control of all variables. When you stop thinking you are in supreme command and give up on that faulty premise, you will be more in charge rather than less in charge.

THE FLIP SIDE OF PRIORITISING

There is, however, the danger of over-prioritising. Being overly dependent may give rise to inflexibility. Getting stuck on one task may inhibit employees from moving on to the next task, resulting in a backlog of uncompleted tasks. If you over plan and over prioritise, you can be paralysed not knowing what comes first or being too caught up in your self imposed structure.

Prioritising incorrectly could lead to a feeling of entitlement. When I was a teenager, I would storm about the house being mad. I have no recollection of what I was mad about, only to embarrassingly suggest that perhaps I was just mad at everything. My mother pulled me aside one day and exclaimed "Look at you! You are walking around as though the whole world owes you a living." She then said, " What you haven't figured out is that you have to work for it." I want to think that I have grown up since then and took that lesson to heart.

When people at work feel entitled, it has a reverberating effect. First off, there is a level of arrogance that somehow they think they deserve things for just showing up. They generally don't believe they should put in the sweat equity. Or even worse, they believe they have when, in essence, they have invested a modicum of effort. For those employees who are entitled the irony is they may never master their work. Oh sure they can get the job done, but they generally want special treatment.

Unless those who present as entitled without priorities change their attitude, they will forever be unhappy not just at work but also in their personal lives. Entitlement is a barrier to mastery of both your work and home life.

It is also important to realise that what you consider to be a top priority is not necessarily everybody else's top priority. Expecting others to share your sense of urgency for a vital task may only happen if they consider it critical. Assuming that everybody has the same priorities is erroneous. When looking for cooperation from others, make sure that you have not just communicated your priorities, but you must also be aware of their priorities. If you are single-minded about your own pressing agenda, your efforts will fall on deaf ears.

Just as flexibility, agility and the ability to pivot are essential when dealing with workplace issues, these same qualities are equally important when setting priorities. Be prepared to make changes and see it not as a failure of completion but rather a need to shift where you spend your energy to get the best results.

ACTION STEPS FOR PRIORITISING

1. Assume priorities will change.

2. Accept that there are many variables at play, many of which are not in your control.

3. Expect that you will need to negotiate, which means your prime concerns may need to be adjusted depending on collective priorities.

4. Do not waste time with what isn't, instead move forward and embrace the new scorecard.

Habit #4

CRITIQUING

*"I think it's very important to have a feedback loop,
where you're constantly thinking about what you've
done and how you could be doing it better."*

~ Elon Musk

Are you doing the right things? Do you ask for feedback on your work? Feedback is critical to allow us to know if we are doing the right things on many fronts. Are we providing high calibre work, are we presenting with influence and impact, are we managing conflict well and many other behaviours that allow us to be successful? If you do not solicit feedback, you will be operating in a dangerous vacuum. You must assume that you can be better at things, be it your communication skills, executive presence, or stakeholding.

It is one of the most humbling things when leaders ask for feedback. It conveys that they don't have all the answers and are seeking to get better. When you can obtain essential data points that make your position more relevant, more accurate or more compelling, you are way more informed. Additionally, by asking for feedback, you make those around you feel good. You demonstrate that you value their opinion, and you want to hear what they have to say. In many ways, there is no greater compliment.

Employees are most often starved for feedback. Many leaders believe that feedback is your salary or the fact that you get to keep your job. That is a severe error in judgment as verbal praise and verbal recognition allow us to know we are on the right track. We want to know that our bosses notice and acknowledge our hard work. Maybe you as a manager do not need feedback, but many of your team members or peers do. It keeps us moving forward in a positive and energised way.

Also, do not assume people can read your mind or know what you need. Be explicit, be transparent. Tell them what you want and if they are not aligned, then explain that. Rather than getting mad or frustrated if you provide respectful guidance, employees will be more than happy to deliver to your expectations. Sometimes we make assumptions that people know what we mean or should "get us". That is faulty thinking, and you end up doing a disservice to them and short change yourself.

To succeed at your job, you need to develop self-awareness, and feedback helps with the process. When you walk through that front door, you convey a certain vibe or energy. It is hard to see what we convey. We think we have a good handle on whether we are approachable, adaptable, solution-oriented, creative, a builder of relationships and many other leadership attributes. I would highly recommend you pick a select number of people at the peer level and a few who are senior and ask them to define your personal brand. Make sure to let them know you are not asking them to be your cheerleaders.

Here is the pivotal question. After the people have provided you with their feedback, ask them if there is one thing you could work on what that would be? Then here is what is going to make the difference. Ask one of the senior individuals to partner with you over the coming months. Whatever that skill is, for example, to be more emotionally resilient or to exude greater self-confidence and let them know you will intermittently ask them if they believe you have moved the needle.

Never underestimate the importance of self-awareness. The greater your self-awareness, the more you will be proficient in every aspect of your work. Ask yourself what your purpose is and once you have clarity, then align your behaviours and efforts in that direction.

It is vital to remember that feedback is a two-way street. It is essential to learn how to receive feedback as well as how to provide it for others. We must understand how to provide input to help others grow and progress. Similarly, we need to be able to accept feedback from others and change our behaviour. Feedback should not be used to assign blame or be regarded as an indictment of one's efforts; instead, it should be viewed as an opportunity to develop and improve.

Foster an open environment where feedback is not just an annual once a year event such as during performance appraisal season but rather a culture of open and ongoing communication.

The Flipside of Critiquing

Too much feedback is onerous. You cannot expect people to change overnight. New behaviours must be practised over and over. It takes a while and many conversations to change behaviour. Place realistic expectations on your team for behaviour change. They likely have been operating this way for many years. Now you are asking for something different. Show benevolence and give them the time and space to make the necessary modifications.

If you fail an endeavour, reflecting and pausing is only of value to a certain point. Make sure in doing so you see failure as a human event. Failure should not be about beating yourself up. When we are too hard on ourselves, we engage in such inner self-criticism, it becomes overbearing. These internal negative thoughts can become debilitating.

Instead, take these self-blaming thoughts and turn them into thoughts of courage, boldness, risk-taking. Dissect what was right in your business plan, what aspects did work well and give yourself credit for the effort and the successful components. Use that as your platform to change your narrative to one of ongoing courage.

Critiquing without a rationale or explanation will not hold water. Explain why you want yourself, direct reports or colleagues to show up differently. They need to understand the context and your rationale. When you provide the basis for your expectations, it allows others to understand and accept your reasoning.

When providing feedback, make sure you do not call out your direct report in front of their peers. This is too often a diminishing habit of some leaders. I suspect they are angry in the moment and let loose. The troubling aspect of a public calling out is that you lose the respect of that employee and the entire team. Only praising should be in public, and calling out should be in private.

Furthermore, the goal is to preserve confidence both within yourself and others. At the end of the day, you decide which of the feedback resonates with your DNA. Which behavioural changes are a good fit for how you are wired? Fitting into a culture must align with your value set and what behaviours you are willing to improve on and which you determine are most relevant to your success.

Action Steps for Critiquing

1. Actively seek feedback. Do so at least once a month because it allows you to calibrate accordingly and is also a good communication opportunity.

2. Provide feedback in a manner that preserves everybody's dignity.

3. Make sure feedback is grounded in examples.

4. Provide the rationale for your ask.

Habit #5

....

IGNITING

"Without a sense of urgency, desire loses its value."

~ Jim Rohn

Creating a feeling of urgency shows the world why your initiatives are essential. It helps if you express yourself with passion and vitality. If you are cerebral and cognitive in approach, you will come across as exacting and not necessarily compelling. You will be making logical and rational arguments, but what will be lost is your ability to ignite your audience. When you convey excitement, you paint a world of possibilities. Your goal is to bring people along. When you inspire others, they will join you on your mission. They become your viral carriers. There is no greater power than the shared power of everyone being engaged in a joint effort.

Everybody loves to escape and dream of a better place. Great speakers fuel their audience with their ability to be great storytellers. By doing so, you take your listener or reader on a journey. They join in by imagining they are there with you. You ignite all their senses. You have catapulted then to a new level. By doing so, you have turned the art of the possible into a reality. They want to be part of this new world, and they want their peers to be so as well. You have lit a spark. They now have become additional fuel, and now you have multiple igniters who collectively carry your message of hope and inspiration.

Annette Verschuren is an esteemed colleague with a striking and diverse business background. Annette exemplifies the ability to fire up her career based upon her ever-growing talents, community interests and philanthropic causes. Annette started her career in the coal mining industry, then went on to privatise crown corporations, worked as an executive for a large holding company, was President of an arts and crafts company expanding their retail reach opening 17 stores within 16 months.

Annette was also President at Home Depot of Canada and Home Depot of Asia where she grew the Canadian operation from 19 to

179 stores between 1996 and 2011. Annette is currently the Chair & CEO of NRStor Inc., an energy storage development company. She is an excellent example of a leader who can take her core business and leadership skills, acquire new knowledge, expertise and further advance her skill set to adapt and be successful to today's and tomorrow's pressing concern for our environment. Her ability to connect with others, listen carefully, be open-minded and excel at stakeholder relations makes her an iconic leader. To top it off, she makes a difference by solving and reducing our carbon footprint through innovative energy storage technologies. What a way to ignite!

THE FLIPSIDE OF IGNITING

Your energy must have substance. If you only lead with your heart, you run the risk of not basing your research on a clear business plan. You will not have done your homework. You will blindly follow your passion thinking you have a brilliant idea. It might be, but does the market really want what you are selling? It doesn't matter how passionate you are or how much you think you have a brilliant concept.

If there is no market for your idea, you will have spent much time, energy, resources and capital in an idea that will never fly. Make sure you bring people into your circle and do the necessary research before you sing the merits of your brave and bold vision. No amount of passion will get you there if not backed by sound business acumen. Convey your business plan and back up your plan with well-researched data.

Also, if you have too much fire in your belly and act with urgency without paying attention to having a work-life balance, you run the risk of burning out.

Action Steps for Igniting

1. Fire up the feeling of urgency to make things happen.

2. Convey your short and concise message through story-telling.

3. Do not speak in a flat or monotone voice; use energy and passion to fuel your vision.

4. Explain to your audience why this matters and why it should matter to them.

Habit #6

. . . .

VISIONING

"The visionary starts with a clean sheet of paper, and re-imagines the world."

~ Malcolm Gladwell

As children, many of us heard the story about the two squirrels. One of them played and played all day. The other one gathered nuts and stored them away for the winter. When winter came, the first squirrel went hungry while the second one thrived. This second squirrel had a vision. He looked to the future, prepared for it, and moved ahead successfully.

In our work, we must also look to the future. It isn't enough to cope with what is happening today. We must also have a vision of what the future will bring and prepare ourselves accordingly. Too many businesses look at their current successes and stay inward-focused. They ride on past wins. Blockbuster did not envision a future where online streaming would render DVD rentals obsolete. Kodak did not anticipate digital photography's impact on the sales of film. Blackberry was not prepared for mobile telephones becoming digital media hubs. Countless retailers held on to their bricks and mortar businesses without thinking ahead until it was too late for them to compete with e-commerce alternatives.

Having a vision of the future doesn't necessarily require having the gifts of a prophet. It does, however, require looking at today's business environment and anticipating what direction it is taking. Having a vision means being prepared to let go of some current assumptions and allow for change. When Ford was the number one automaker in the world and was selling more Model-T's than they could build, GM started offering cars in a wide variety of colours. Henry Ford famously responded to the consumer demand for different colours by saying, "They can have my car in any colour they want, as long as it's black." This lack of vision and rigid outlook dropped Ford out of its number one position, a ranking that they have never recovered.

Having a vision is not limited to major strategic initiatives; it can be as simple as understanding that there will be a market for computer keyboards with over-sized letters and numbers with an ever aging population. To get ahead and be assigned projects with greater scope, your bosses, peers, and those who are senior need to know who you are and what value you bring.

Being strategic is not only envisioning your company's future; it is also about being strategic about your career. Make sure that you build important relationships that run across the enterprise. If you make the mistake of hanging out with your usual cast of characters, then likely your network is too small. To be known is to be valued and to be valued is equated with ever-increasing roles of importance.

People often become anxious when they are told to be more strategic. It doesn't mean that you have to invent the next source of renewable energy or develop a more effective way to explore outer space. It may mean that you can establish more efficient or practical ways of doing business. You may have removed costs, cut down response times, or sped up distribution channels. These are all innovative practices.

It means understanding that "We've always done it that way." is not a reason to keep doing things that way. Having a vision means being willing to listen to input from others. Having a vision means looking at ways to retain your current consumer base and anticipating who will be your future customers.

THE FLIPSIDE OF VISIONING

When looking ahead, we must take care not to sacrifice what we already have. Some visionaries can become so caught up in looking to the future they ignore their current business. They become distracted and stop focusing on enhancing their existing product line and customer base. Looking to tomorrow does not permit us to ignore today. We must be able to strike a balance between taking care of today's business and being forward-thinking.

Efficiencies, distribution channels, improving your current product line requires strengthening your current business proposition. Make sure you never take your eye off the ball. By just focusing on your moon shot, you risk abandoning your critical legacy.

ACTION STEPS FOR VISIONING

1. Think about the future. How can your business stay relevant?

2. Keep a close ear to the ground to watch market trends.

3. Recognise it is not you, but rather the consumer, that has all the power. Listen to what they want and desire.

4. Create a sound business plan rather than riding on the romance of an idea.

Habit #7

. . . .

PIVOTING

"Progress is impossible without change; and those who cannot change their minds cannot change anything."

~ George Bernard Shaw

The very best leaders are fluid, adapt and transition their skills depending upon the personalities they are leading and the nature of the business they are in. Whether you are a star athlete or a successful business leader, you must be able to adapt and adjust your skillset to the new and ever-growing array of competitive pressures. It means acting based on vision and data to adapt to improvement.

Many businesses became defunct because they could not adapt to the changing circumstances around them and pivot towards a successful path. As time changes, people become more knowledgeable and want different things.

For example, with new knowledge emerging daily around pollution and climate change caused by extracting and burning fossil fuels, many energy companies are pivoting towards renewables.

Mastering how to pivot should matter to you. What is okay is to have different drivers that may underlie why you want to accomplish targeted goals. For some, it's about pride and honour, for others, it's about getting to the next level and doing what is necessary to keep their job.

Society makes value statements around more allegedly being better. In other words being more senior, striving for more money, being more powerful through career advancement, being an iconic trailblazer. You should not fall into that trap or be pulled in by societal pressures if, in fact, those things are not important to you in your heart. Society might judge you if you are happy in your role and have no further ambitions. Maybe you are content to be with one employer for your entire career.

What is important when it comes to mastery is pivoting towards what you really want out of work. Once you know this and are comfortable, that becomes your guiding principle. It actually is liberating as you do not have to fall into the vortex of what society or anybody else suggests you be. How freeing is that?

Many companies have pivoted by expanding their offerings to stay relevant and create additional revenue streams. Amazon was originally a distributor for books only. Now they sell a multitude of products and are the largest e-commerce company in the world. Netflix initially started similar to Blockbuster, and then they began streaming films, now they produce their own content. Given that many people enjoy the comforts of their home to access products and entertainment at the tip of their fingertips. Technology platforms allow us to enjoy a better quality of life. This cuts down on travel time and expenses, creates a highly competitive market place and for some, enhances work-life balance. In turn, we have more time to divide which way to pivot.

Gianna Manes was the CEO of Enmax, a public utility for eight years. She inherited an organisation that was in significant need of a brand and cultural change. The shareholder, the city and consumers looked to Gianna to transform the organisation and win back public confidence. One of her key mandates was to pivot a public utility creating opportunities for growth and efficiency.

The day my phone rang, and Gianna was at the other end was a true honour. What emerged was and remains to this very day a hallmark of Gianna's pivoting style. She began our interaction with "I need your help". I knew right there that we would forge a great long-term relationship. It was a privilege to work with Gianna and her leadership team to transform the organisation where employees felt proud to be a part of a prosperous and growing company.

No small feat as during Gianna's reign there was a city fire creating significant operational risk, municipal elections, a city wide flood, a shrinking oil and gas sector, and a downturn in the economy. Yet she still managed to lead Enmax's first-ever utility acquisition with success.

Every open and transparent leader will tell you that the stress of the role cannot be underestimated and fully appreciated until you are no longer in the role. As a CEO of a public utility owned by a municipality, there is also the complexity of the shareholder and the city councillors. In addition to the board, the CEO requires a sophisticated level of skills to appeal, negotiate, and respond to multiple stakeholders.

Gianna and I worked together to identify and grow talent, develop successors, act as a sounding board for strategic plans and be a trusted advisor. It was so very clear that Gianna exemplified the humble confidence that inspires others to be the very best and adapt to all kinds of scenarios life may throw our way.

I watched Gianna in many forums, including her senior executive team, board presentations and organisation-wide town halls. Gianna never came into any dialogue from a formal or informal perspective, assuming she had all the answers. She asked tough and pointed questions, making sure she understood the complexity of the challenges before her. For those who partnered with her, it was a heady experience. Everyone at her table was treated as an expert. She mined their intelligence and solicited their point of view. What was equally compelling was that she would go away and reflect on the newly found information with the intent to pivot more successfully.

When she came back, it wasn't ever about needing Gianna to agree with you. In fact, you respected that she had her reasons, some of which you were not privy to, for making certain decisions. After all, each of us has a lens, but the CEO must have multiple lenses that include the employee population, stakeholders, the board, the consumer, the shareholder and the balance sheet. I challenge you to try on this job. No small task. Sure it appears glamorous to run an organisation and be the CEO; however, you can never underestimate the role's enormity and supreme responsibility. Gianna possesses a remarkable combination of instilling confidence along with a quest for knowledge and learning to make the best and most informed decisions for adapting. If I had to choose a boss, Gianna would be mine. But I am far luckier than that, Gianna is a colleague and friend.

Leaders who adapt can reap the benefit of having many careers and impacting in so many ways.

THE FLIPSIDE OF PIVOTING

History shows that people and organisations have often pivoted based on inaccurate information or conspiracy theories. Adapting because of non-truthful information can be dangerous and fact-checking is a must before deciding to shift in a new direction. It helps if you surround yourself with thought leaders who have their pulse on where the industry is going. Being nimble enough to promote that you are a leader who thrives on adaptation is only of value if you are plugged into the zeitgeist of where the economy, technology and the market are headed. Make sure you adapt with purpose and intent.

ACTION STEPS FOR PIVOTING

1. Think about your own personality. Are you someone who likes to challenge the status quo? Or do you continue to do things as you always have? If it is the latter, you need to invite change.

2. Seek out uncomfortable scenarios. Ask to be put on a new project.

3. Surround yourself with big picture thinkers. Watch how they approach life. See how they think and unpack today's challenges.

4. Find a peer who can challenge your thinking and push you to be more future-oriented.

Habit #8

ENJOYING

"Carpe diem! Rejoice while you are alive; enjoy the day; live life to the fullest; make the most of what you have. It is later than you think."

~ Horace

Y ou know those individuals who say "I never worked a day in my life". Don't you just envy those colleagues? They love going to work; they see their careers as having flown by and get up each morning with positive momentum.

Sounds too good to be true? Not really, this could also be you. Here's the first step. Never do something because someone suggested it would be a promising career for you. Do they really and truly know you? Or are they projecting their biases and dreams upon you? They might mean well and have good intentions, but you need to personally sort out your habit of enjoying.

I often ask people how they came into their careers. It is interesting to hear how many people have chosen their careers by default. Well, their neighbour was an insurance broker, so they landed them an interview with a major insurance company. They had an uncle who worked for an auto manufacturer and many other similar scenarios. Maybe you even recognise yourself in these stories.

When we are in school and study career choices, it is hard to really know how they will translate to real life. Working as a scientist to find a cure for cancer sounds noble, and it is. But maybe you love the outdoors and sitting in a lab all day is not your thing. How can we really know what we want out of our careers or even the career type we should have?

Take me, for example. After three years as an employee, I knew I would continue to fail as an employee. I grew up in a family of all self-employed individuals. That was my model. Following other people's processes, rules, and procedures weren't my thing. It took me a while to learn that being self-employed fit me the best and for over two-plus decades continues to bring me much fulfilment.

The first step is to be both patient and realistic. Very few of us begin our careers and land the jackpot of happiness and fulfilment.

It could help if you find out what you are good at, what you excel at. This will take a few tries and a few flops. Maybe you thought spending all day with spreadsheets figuring out algorithms would be exciting then you realise that you miss the energy of others and sitting in front of your screen all day just doesn't cut it. So you then need to pause, reflect and regroup. Try something else.

When you find your groove, then it doesn't mean that there isn't stress. Of course there is. Our worlds never go according to plan. There are roadblocks, snags, and annoying and challenging personalities all along the way. But here's the deal. When you enjoy what you do, then this serves as immunisation. Having fun allows you to get inoculated against stressors. You still feel them and need to find a way to respond constructively, but the override is the fulfilment you get when you enjoy what you do. The key is to establish and cultivate a sense of mastery. When you do that, your job, despite hard work, comes with ease. You are now an expert. People flock to you. You now have what they want. It is exceptionally infectious. You are doubly rewarded. You enjoy what you do, and feel rewarded by the enthusiasm and appreciation of others who genuinely value your skillset.

THE FLIPSIDE OF ENJOYING

Make sure though that you remain self-governing in your pursuit of play at work. If you have too much fun, you run the risk of being too playful. Self-governance is essential to allow you to stay focused, disciplined and on track. Enjoying what you do still must involve setting milestones and assigning key metrics that track your timelines and goals. You cannot afford to get sloppy, cavalier or indulgent. Always track against yourself as well as the competition.

Stay outwardly focused as you will need to keep your pulse on what the market is telling you they want. Just because you are having fun does not mean that you are current. Make sure you are staying relevant based upon what the consumer is saying they want and need.

Action Steps for Enjoying

1. Expect that it is unlikely that your very first job or even your first few jobs end up being your ultimate career path.

2. Think about what you love to do. What brings you joy?

3. What type of environment do you need? Do you feed off the energy of others? Or do you prefer a solitary environment?

4. Do you want to work for a not for profit and feel part of a community effort? Or do you prefer to work within a large for-profit organisation?

Habit #9

DIFFERENTIATING

"If you are always trying to be normal, you will never know how amazing you can be."

~ Maya Angelou

Often, we hear a cliche along the lines of, "be more original", but what does being original mean?

Differentiating is an essential habit for self-development and thinking outside of the box. Bringing different yet highly creative ideas to the table will make you stand out. Differentiating is a leadership trait often observed in change makers who are great at pre-conceiving trends through educated guesses.

How can you differentiate better? Could it be your unique presence? Or your original ideas? Maybe some other trait? In essence, what is your personal brand? Ask yourself this fundamental question. How do you bring value in ways that either your peers or other leaders have not been able to? Think about solving a problem in a way that has not been approached or implemented before.

Most successful companies in the 21st Century promote and reinforce the idea of differentiation and are taking action by hiring Chief Diversity and Inclusion Officers to change the talent pool. They are under enormous scrutiny by boards to differentiate their organisational makeup. There are very few companies that are not focused or under the gun for Diversity Equity Inclusion initiatives. These initiatives sadly are a much needed and long overdue initiative.

The Flipside of Differentiating

There is a fine line between being different and being an outsider. Differentiation has value when you can separate yourself from group think. It is essential to get recognised as the different insider; otherwise, you could come across as an irritating attention seeker. To differentiate yourself without offering substantive ways of looking at problem resolution will not hold water. In other words, your differentiation should be about how your talent adds a new or different type of currency that brings a unique and challenging perspective. How do you challenge the status quo to bring about much-needed change?

Thinking against the grain could get you into trouble sometimes, so it is essential to be selective about how you go about using this habit when working on meaningful projects and managing your reputation.

ACTION STEPS FOR DIFFERENTIATING

1. Think about your personal brand. How can you define it to make a difference compared to your peers?

2. When describing what makes you unique, don't summarise your resume. Instead, demonstrate how your skills are uniquely positioned to solve your organisation's most pressing problems.

3. Create and promote a 2-3 minute sound bite that defines your unique value proposition.

4. Think of ways to differentiate all of your projects.

Habit #10

LEARNING

"The illiterate of the 21st century will not be those who cannot read and write, but those who cannot learn, unlearn, and relearn."

~ Alvin Toffler

Gaining new knowledge is often the best kind of investment a person can make for their future. Whether it be from reading books, signing up to a new education programme, or taking up a new skill. After all, what you are doing now falls under learning too. It helps if you consider yourself as a lifetime student. Stay up to date with what changes and advances are occurring in your field and other fields. The best leaders study other disciplines for inspiration be it literary influences, the arts, artificial intelligence and many other areas of study. These learnings open your mind to view problems in different ways. This provides stimulation for your own professional world.

Learners continually ask good questions. They do not make assumptions but rather ask questions to learn and grow. By asking good questions, you gain more information, engage in debate and sharpen your thinking. The ultimate goal is to continue to grow your thinking and never to stagnate.

In addition to helping, you keep on top of your field, learning can also open entirely new fields for you. A colleague working in marketing took a financial management course for non-financial managers since she had never been exposed to finance before and felt that this course would give her a better appreciation for some of her finance-related aspects of work. She discovered an unanticipated passion for finance. Her career trajectory deviated dramatically from where it was initially pointed, and she explored and found a plethora of new opportunities in the area of finance. Indeed, additional learning in her new field was instrumental in her further development and progress.

THE FLIP SIDE OF LEARNING

Your learning, be it a course, reading or skill acquisition must turn into action. There is a point when you must concede that you will never have all the information, nor will you have necessarily perfected your new skill. Do not strive for perfection in your zeal for learning. You will never get there because you will keep raising the bar. Self-imposed pressure is of value as long as you can connect it with a call to action. Stay current but ensure you are not stuck in the rut of needing to know everything. You need to take your new-found knowledge and turn that into tangible efforts. Efforts that produce measurable results.

ACTION STEPS FOR LEARNING

1. Make a point of looking through the courses or programs offered by the colleges and universities in your community and online offerings.

2. Sign up for a course that allows you to enhance your current skill set or that helps you to develop a new skill.

3. If you manage people, encourage your team members to also look for and sign up for learning opportunities.

4. Take action based on the notes you take from learning.

Habit #11

RISK-TAKING

"Nothing ventured, nothing gained."

~ Geoffrey Chaucer

L iterature and lore are full of praise for risk-takers. It is important to remember that although risk can result in reward, it can also lead to loss and painful consequences. Risk-taking in the workplace requires sound judgment, the ability to assess the risk level, and the willingness to take a well-calculated leap to achieve growth.

Risk-takers look at the available information and based on their experience, expertise, and judgement, commit to a direction. Those whose decisions are right more often than not will succeed and progress in their careers. Those who are unwilling to take a risk may never make a mistake, nor experience any great success. They will excel at keeping the lights on. Every organisation requires these Steady Eddie's.

However, the ability to engage in well thought out risk is a crucial requirement for leaders who are game-changers. Adopting new technology, launching a new product, making a new hire, joining a start-up company are all decisions that engender risk. They are also decisions that have the potential for great reward. Being able to make balanced decisions and overcome the fear of risk makes the world a better place. Risk-taking is along a continuum of evolution or revolution. Either way, you advance society, and that is a great thing.

Risk takers are the ones who blaze the trail that everybody else follows. Everybody who is the first to do something has taken a risk. In 1968, South African Christiaan Barnard was the first surgeon to perform a heart transplant. Today, thousands of these surgeries are performed all over the world. This risk-taker paved the way for all who followed. In 1903 the Wright brothers took the first powered flight. That flight lasted just a few seconds, but it paved the way for today's trans-continental and trans-oceanic flights. Every discovery, each new business launch, and every investment of time or money involves some risk element, which is a necessary element of progress.

Risk-taking requires a certain amount of self-confidence and boldness. Here is a story about when I was flying home from Fayetteville, Arkansas, with a colleague. My colleague is 6 feet 2 inches tall and lean. I am 5 feet 1 inches tall, and that's on a good day. Typically, when I board a plane, I generally don't abide by the zoned boarding instructions. I prefer to board early and skip the queue so that I don't have to climb over everyone and there is a good spot for my luggage in the overhead bin. My colleague and I were assigned to Zone 5, and when they called for passengers in Zone 2, I said, "Come on, let's board." He replied, "We can't. They didn't call our zone." I said, "Oh, it doesn't matter; we'll be fine." He said, "I'm really not comfortable with that." To which I replied, "Come on. It's not as though I'm asking you to break the law." He followed behind me sheepishly. When we got to the gate, the flight attendant said to me, "Welcome aboard. Enjoy your flight." As I boarded the plane, my colleague was next, and I heard the flight attendant saying to him, "Sir, we haven't called your zone yet. Please step aside." I laughed all the way to my seat. This is an excellent example of exhibiting confidence, convincing others you belong and owning your space.

THE FLIPSIDE OF RISK-TAKING

We must, however, guard against making risky decisions just for the sake of risk. Some people feed on risk as an adrenaline rush. They have a low threshold for boredom, need to stir things up and sometimes seek out drama. They may look at the potential reward without weighing it against the downside of failure. If one risky decision fails, rather than re-group, they may make an even riskier decision to recoup their losses, much like a gambler who throws good money after bad.

Risk-taking in the workplace is positive as long as the risks are based on well-founded information, clear thinking, and a sound assessment of the decision's pros and cons. We like to call it cautious risk-taking.

ACTION STEPS FOR RISK-TAKING

1. Look for opportunities to make decisions or take actions which are outside of your traditional comfort zone.

2. In looking at these opportunities, before going ahead, conduct a risk assessment by looking at the pros and cons, the likelihood of success, and the repercussions of failure.

3. Use your analysis to make and justify a go/no-go decision.

4. Focus on the good risks and eliminate any bad ones.

Habit #12
. . . .
SELF-PROMOTING

"It's not bragging if you can back it up."

~ Muhammad Ali

73

It's essential to do the work, but you must also find ways to promote your achievements; otherwise, you might not get noticed. The person who shouts the loudest may not necessarily have done the most work or have had the most significant impact; however, creating visibility and profile is vital to be recognised for your achievements.

Self-promotion has traditionally had negative connotations. It can be seen as grandstanding or grabbing a front-row seat. Moving down from the bleachers can be viewed as opportunistic. And what is actually wrong with being opportunistic?

It helps if you believe in yourself because you then create a profile. If you stay on the sidelines, you do not promote visibility. Please do not make the all-too-common mistake of thinking your work speaks for itself. Lots of people do good work. We assume that is why you were hired. You have the talent or skill set to do the job. That though is your entry ticket. You must boast in a humble way to get the attention you deserve.

You need to find ways to be visible. Ask your manager if you can present at his or her boss's table. This presence will allow your boss's supervisor and peers to see your contribution, how you carry yourself, how you answer challenging questions and your bigger picture thinking.

Sometimes taking the mantra of TEAM can eclipse that you were the architect or chief driver of the project. Boasting can be done elegantly; it conveys confidence that you believe in what you are doing and that you are a true leader. Influence and impact involves being able to move or convince colleagues of the merit of your position. If you show passion, conviction and a belief in yourself and what you are doing, you are seen as a winner. Who doesn't want to be associated with a winner?

Remaining quiet will lead others to misjudge your contribution. You might get marginalised and your value could be diminished. And guess what? If you have more senior aspirations, you must be viewed as a leader who can lead change. Most people are change-resistant so boasting about your achievements, showcasing mountains you have moved, and wins that you have had illustrates that you can effect change and be a true thought leader.

One of the critical questions senior executives ask is whether you have the confidence to navigate challenging personalities. The higher you go in an organisation, it is often the case that seasoned and accomplished individuals got there because of their grit and ability to negotiate what they believe brings value.

THE FLIPSIDE OF SELF-PROMOTING

When you boast too much, then you are downright obnoxious. You will alienate others. You will be perceived as having your own agenda. You run the risk of running your own race. The best definition of a narcissist is someone who likes to operate both the projector and the screen at the same time.

Being a blowhard guarantees you will have retention problems. No one wants their brand to be affected by a grandstander. Be careful. If you stay within an ego-driven leader's orbit, you run the risk of never being given the light of day, and if you are the pompous leader, you will attract sycophants who do as you say and will never challenge you. This failure to act means you will likely work in a vacuum divorced from fresh and new thinking. People want to have a voice, and they deserve to have a seat at the table. If you drown them out, you will find yourself alone in an empty room. Now that's a dangerous equation.

ACTION STEPS FOR SELF-PROMOTING

1. Be selective around when and how often you self-promote. Too much exposure is the equivalent of posting so often on social media that you saturate your audience.

2. When you claim your victory, explain some of the challenges along the way. Make your journey real. Don't pretend it was a slam dunk.

3. Explain how others helped shape and enhance your thinking.

4. Find your voice along with opportunities to present internally within your organisation and at industry conferences.

Habit #13

FOCUSING

"Whenever you want to achieve something, keep your eyes open, concentrate and make sure you know exactly what it is you want. No one can hit their target with their eyes closed."

~ Paulo Coelho

The word focus is commonly associated with photography. When we think of a photo that is in focus, we think of a crisp image showing us a clear representation of the photographer's view. Conversely, when we look at an image that is badly out of focus, it can be hard to discern what we are seeing. The certainty of the focused picture stands in stark contrast to the ambiguity that results from a lack of focus. Just as focus is essential for a good photograph, it is also a key element for success in the workplace. Lack of focus can ruin a picture, and it can derail a career. You can learn how to focus a camera, and you can also learn how to focus on your goals.

Think about what it means to focus on your work. For example, when you publish something on social media, forget what people say in the comments unless it is constructive criticism. Instead, focus on your next task at hand. It is also crucial to focus more on yourself than the competition if you genuinely want to create breakthroughs. At the same time, it is essential to focus on the competition from a market research perspective.

Using another photography analogy, we must realise that we can select from several different lenses when we focus. If we use too narrow a focus, we may lose sight of the big picture. Maintaining your focus should not narrow your perspective. Instead, it should broaden your outlook and give you a clearer vision of where you are and where you are heading.

Focusing requires patience. Exercises like meditation and playing games requiring mind-based focus skills can help boost this habit. In todays' complex world with shortened attention spans we must ensure we do not miss out on important details.

I recall sitting down with a colleague at the beginning of the year. I asked him what his goals or objectives were for the year ahead.

He replied, "My number one objective is to get a promotion". His response was not at all unusual. When I speak with executives, this irks them. They see that aspiration based upon status or title rather than seeking to make a difference.

It helps if your ambitiousness is tied to carving out something beyond your expected scope. Examples might include successfully launching a new product, surpassing sales targets, introducing and integrating new technology, or generating new revenue streams. When you add this kind of value, your ability to be recognised will be equated with career advancement and a likely promotion.

Most great jobs are the result of having a deep attention to detail. Whether it be Da Vinci's Mona Lisa painting or St. Paul's Cathedral in the heart of London, UK, one must regularly build on the habit of looking at more delicate details and reflecting it within your own work.

THE FLIPSIDE OF FOCUSING

Over focusing can result in analysis paralysis where you may think too much and not act at all. You may at times experience significant self doubt. It is vital to balance all of your habits and always work on focusing in enjoyable ways. Ask yourself: How can I make focusing more fun?

Another flipside to focusing is if you go over the top with your attention to detail. There is no such thing as perfection, only excellence and continuous improvement. So you must be able to recognise when a piece of work is excellent enough to call it a day.

ACTION STEPS FOR FOCUSING

1. At the start of each day, pause and think about one or two priorities for the day that you want to accomplish.

2. Think about what you need to do to accomplish these items.

3. At the end of the day, assess your performance relative to these tasks.

4. Try exercises that build your patience and focus your mind.

Habit #14

CARING

"Nobody cares how much you know, until they know how much you care."

~ Theodore Roosevelt

Leading with your heart matters. We always speak of leaders needing to adjust to the economic landscape or competitive pressures. What is also so very important is a leader's ability to showcase empathy. This takes many forms. I am often asked, "Well, how many leadership styles do I need to have?" Our answer is as many as the number of people that you lead. In other words, every one of us has individual drivers, backgrounds, interpersonal styles. This means to bring out the best in others you need to take the time to understand each person you work with, what makes them happy, what gets them frustrated.

I recall one of my clients was the COO of an organisation, and she said to me "Everybody has roles, responsibilities and targets. Why do I need to ask them about how their weekend was or how they are adjusting to their new house, baby or brand-new puppy?" She said, "Isn't there a division between work and home?" I, of course, was shocked and dismayed. I explained to her that yes, there must be boundaries between one's work and personal life. However, if everyone feels like a worker and not a human being with a personal life filled with other interests, responsibilities and stressors, they won't feel cared for as people. I explained that based on their own work ethic or value set they may still produce good work however if she was looking for them to go the extra mile or work for her for hopefully a long time, that was an unlikely proposition.

If you as a leader don't show empathy, then you will be seen as a taskmaster. Everyone on your team will feel like everyone else. Additionally, when we show care for others, then people in our team feel valued and respected as unique individuals. They are grateful for being treated as human beings with personal lives that are accompanied by stressors and family priorities. Taking the time to ask your team how they feel and how they are managing goes a long way. It shows you care, and you are being sensitive.

That kind of care builds loyalty. Your team will want to work for you. They will put in top tier effort because they feel they matter beyond just a machine doing a job but as whole human beings with lives outside of work.

Empathy also means self-care. If you do not put boundaries around your work, you are setting yourself up for an unhealthy scenario. We all need to be refuelled and replenished. Feeding your mind and body through good nutrition, exercise and diverse interests will allow you to be a productive contributor with fresh energy and perspective. You want to be a good role model for others where you convey the values of self-care. Otherwise, you will burn yourself and your team out, resulting in stress leaves or terminations.

THE FLIPSIDE OF CARING

Too much empathy can be a liability in that you run the risk of having too much heart. A leader still needs to make tough decisions. No matter how much you invest in a team member; they still may not make the mark. You need to cut your losses, as these people are either not constructive, not adding value, or are making too many mistakes. Your business cannot afford this. There are other times where you might need to restructure, and job action is required. These are tough decisions impacting people's family and finances. Your team will respect you for making the right business decision rather than preserving low hanging fruit or skill sets that are no longer of value.

ACTION STEPS FOR CARING

1. Take the time to get to know your team. Ask them about their families, their interests, how they spend their free time.

2. Spend time understanding what they like about their job, what they find stressful and support them with their career goals.

3. Send them a note or give them a shout out when they have done exceptional work or gone the extra mile.

4. Remember to care for yourself and organisation too.

Habit #15
BELIEVING

"You may be the only person left who believes in you, but it's enough. It takes just one star to pierce a universe of darkness. Never give up."

~ Richelle E. Goodrich

If you don't believe in yourself, then no one else will. You must believe in yourself and your capabilities. When you don't, this speaks to imposter syndrome. When you don't believe in yourself, and when you have success or achievements, imposters tend to externalise their wins. They attribute their success to external factors. "It must be luck, somebody else was responsible", or "I was at the right place, at the right time." You have every excuse to explain away your achievements. This is a shame as it also comes across as a victim. A victim and a passive bystander. Think about this. No company hired you because they are benevolent. You are not a poster child for a cause. You are hired for what you bring to the table.

Also, think about your past wins. There is generally a common thread. Although each challenge is different, you could not be just smart once, and of course you aren't. So, in essence, your ongoing achievements are built on previous successes. You did not become unsmart or less smart. On the contrary.

Think about the mistakes you have made. Have any of them truly been significant, or are they minor with important learnings? Stop beating yourself up. Do not set perfection as a standard. Perfectionists never win because they are always comparing themselves to others. You do have a choice: to set the bar high and be happy with your accomplishments. Positive performance appraisals, bonuses, raises, and promotions are earned and deserved. No one feels sorry for you. You have made a difference based on merit.

Being patient and believing in yourself and your team members allows for meaningful insights. On the way back from a trip on behalf of a client, I sat in the airport lounge with my colleague. He sat on many boards, and I asked him to explain why he thought he was so successful and why he was sought after as an opinion leader. His answer might surprise you; it surely surprised me. He said it was hard to really know as he sincerely believed he shared many of the same attributes as everybody else such as hard work, determination, and a creative mindset. When I pressed him for more, he postulated that perhaps his success was his ability to see positive attributes that others did not see in themselves. He indicated that he believed many employees might be in roles that were not playing to their strengths. They were, in essence, not happy at what they were doing and felt stuck. He instituted a rotational program where every employee could rotate or have an assignment from each department be it Human Resources, Finance, Merchandising, IT, and so on.

As a leader at work, it is your job to find ways to bring out the best in others. Do not make the mistake of giving up on your team members too soon. If they fail, a number of times, it is not the individual who fails but the organisation's failure in providing a chance for them to excel.

We all want to be inspired. We want to surround ourselves with positive energy. We as humans feed off others. When you believe in yourself, then you attract people who want to be on your team. Positive energy emboldens us. When you see yourself as a star, then others shine bright as well.

Malala Yousafzai believes in herself and the right for females to have the same voice and opportunities as males in parts of the world where this is not the norm. The passion of her belief and her convictions has made her into one of the most prominent voices in the world for the promotion of equal rights. As a result of her raising awareness throughout the world, she was awarded the Nobel Peace Prize and became the youngest Nobel laureate in history.

Your personality disposition also matters regarding how and when you will achieve a sense of mastery. When we look at optimists, they can be critiqued for not being in touch with reality. I think this cannot be further from the truth. Would you not choose to be on an optimist's team over a glass half empty team?

When people whine, they are negative. They are like solar panels, sucking the energy out of the room. However, they too attract people; generally, they form groups of injustice collectors—individuals who complain and waste good energy rather than acting towards positive change.

Optimists believe that obstacles can be overcome with the right kind of effort, resources, and never taking no for an answer. Think about how you see and interface with the world. How you face each day is a direct correlation to your outcomes for the day. Bad stuff happens, annoying people get in our way and challenges abound.

When you go to bed at night, you might be discouraged. You can learn to shake this off and instead put on a cloak of optimism. It is your choice, and it is a superpower that can propel you from a sense of helplessness to true empowerment.

The Flipside of Believing

Don't get all heady. When you believe too much in yourself, then you have decided you are the smartest person in the room. You run the danger of being seen as egocentric. When this happens, I advise employees to change rooms. Too much of you and your views discourages debate and the ability to challenge and grant permission to have new ideas. Check your ego at the door. The right balance is humble confidence. This means you can be self-assured while at the same time acknowledging when you are wrong and need to switch gears.

Never ask for permission. If you do, you may be waiting in line, and your turn will never come. Furthermore, why put your faith in someone else's hands. If you have a bold idea on improving processes, increasing your customer base, creating multiple channels, or developing new technologies and wait for permission, your opportunity will most likely be missed. If you are working within a large organisation, bureaucracy will slow you down. Instead, you should put together a small committee or task force and implement a pilot. Once you have a successful template, it becomes easier to sell your vision on a bigger scale.

Being bold is having the courage to fly against those who will either be threatened by your foresight, see things as too complicated, or are just plain lazy. Pushing ahead is being truthful to your convictions. When you stay true to your beliefs, your sense of purpose is unwavering. This level of fortitude safeguards your success.

Action Steps for Believing

1. Look at the facts. Your wins are based on the targets you have achieved.

2. Think about the relationships you have fostered. Likely you are respected, and it is why your peers will do things on your behalf.

3. Are you sought out for your opinion and point of view?

4. Say thank you and express gratitude when you are complimented. Own your wins. Do not diminish your offerings.

Habit #16

PERSISTING

"Failing up and making mistakes is an essential part of developing."

~ Cindy Wahler

S tuff happens. Temperament matters as many variables could go wrong; be it people, technical, or economic challenges. If you are rigid, think in a linear way, or have a volatile demeanour, you will have trouble navigating.

You need to engage in due diligence and anticipate all variables. Contingency planning is also crucial; however, no matter how much you plan, you cannot forecast the future. Whether world events impact the company, resources are scarce, and distribution channels dry up, a wrong hire or many other unforeseen events, this will put a monkey wrench in your plans. If you cannot show resolve by regrouping, then you message to your team that dealing with instability is something you cannot manage. This will undermine the confidence your team has in you.

I recall a client of mine was very passionate and brought tremendous enthusiasm to his role. On a good day, he instilled tremendous momentum in his team. His leadership style though was inconsistent. There were days he earned the title appointed by his employees who called him "Mount Vesuvius." This led his team to give up and disengage. They took his excitement and outward yelling as an inability to stay the course. They exclaimed, "If our own boss has given up and does not have the stamina or fortitude how then can we?" Sadly, they lost confidence in his ability to take them through tumultuous times.

Great leaders anticipate that things will change. Even though they do not always know what will change, they are prepared to pull their team together and regroup. This allows both you, the leader, and your team to be resourceful. The goal is to foster creativity. Brainstorming together is exhilarating, and there is no greater reward than finding new pathways. What appears daunting and impossible after much dialogue leads to a path of recovery or a new direction. The best leaders earn trust and credibility, connecting people to their vision who ultimately are their culture carriers.

Leaders who scream and yell or retreat behind closed doors demonstrate poor leadership. It means they cannot cope with a shifting landscape. People look to leaders for confidence that the organisation will reposition itself and they will get there. You are not expected to have all the answers immediately, but you are expected to demonstrate that you will help create a path forward. Directs look to you for reassurance. They want to know everything will be alright. Engaging in reaching solutions together with a calm demeanour shows important stewardship.

One of my clients was exceptionally frustrated when she saw that her colleagues were being promoted year after year, and she continually was passed over. Furthermore, when she applied to three different internal roles, she was turned down. I advised her to go and find out why she was not a successful candidate. Thankfully one of the executives was transparent and told her that the hiring committee did not know who she really was. She was incredulous and somewhat offended. Leading one of the largest transformation projects for her organisation, she was considered highly successful as she had come in under budget and finished six months earlier than projected.

The executive told her yes, of course, but we don't really know who you are. Instead of representing yourself, you always sent one of your team members or a peer. Furthermore, you turned down every invitation to join us for dinner to discuss challenges and future opportunities. This lesson was essential and influential regarding others determining your fate even when you do outstanding work.

You can't give up the first time you take a fall. It is a myth to believe that people or their businesses are an overnight success. It may appear that way or the media loves to suggest it is so. Entrepreneurs or change-makers fail many times before becoming successful in their endeavours. There are good reasons for this, and more importantly, failing upwards is critical to your success.

First off, you have an idea. No matter how great your idea is, it still is a thought or a concept. You need to test the concept and see whether it is the right concept. Do you have buy-in, will it work, is there a market? This also applies to how we lead and work with others. I am sure most of us are not proud of how we have handled certain interpersonal interactions. Maybe we were too harsh, maybe not strong enough or maybe we presented in a way that was ineffectual or didn't resonate.

Here is the litmus test. If you reflect on your career, surely you can think of scenarios where you would handle a situation differently today. In other words, you are expected to fail. If you have courage, that means you will fail. Having courage means you are bold and will take chances. Taking chances means you don't truly know until you try.

The cool thing is that once you try and you have failed you now have new data points. So do not be beleaguered. There is no need to stay down for long. Dust yourself off, take the failure as a learning moment. Stand tall and try again. Keep trying because with each failure, you are wiser. This combination of failure and new wisdom will put you on the path to success.

The Flipside of Persisting

If you are too resilient, you will appear robotic or uncaring. Too much confidence will be seen as being potentially dismissive and undermine the importance of the challenge. Being responsive and caring to both the situation and your team's fears shows you are on top of this. You want to demonstrate that you are sensitive to their worries but also convey you see the horizon.

There is a point though that you may need to make a call if you have failed many times. Speak to experts in your chosen field and see what they have to say. You may need to cut bait. You may need to decide that there isn't a market for your idea. Take pride in your efforts and regroup. Put that persistence to good use in another way.

You are admirable for your tenacity; however, you need to make sure you are not tone deaf or do not suffer from tunnel vision. Take those great traits of devotion and commitment and step back. Think about how you can apply those skills differently or to a new and fresh idea. Don't take it personally. Do not see yourself as a failure. Rather it is part of the process, and many factors are not in your control. What is in your control is your ability to re-group and re-engage your energy in a different pursuit.

ACTION STEPS FOR PERSISTING

1. Recognise that the road will be bumpy.

2. Create a contingency plan.

3. Seek outside counsel.

4. Brainstorm with your team so you can consider alternative approaches.

Habit #17

....

CONDITIONING

"And once you understand that habits can change, you have the freedom and the responsibility to remake them."

~ Charles Duhigg

Forcing yourself to get into new habits until you become accustomed to them requires discipline but the payoff is often worth it. Once you've acquired a certain skill set or habit, muscle memory takes over, and it becomes a part of your lifestyle. For example, a person who learns to drive a car or ride a bicycle never forgets how to do it.

The twenty habits mentioned in this book could be a starting point for your conditioning journey. Following that, you could ask yourself, "Which new skills or habits can I condition myself to learn?"

The habits required to succeed in the workplace should become second nature to you. There are many skills required in the workplace that can be practised and become part of your conditioning for success. For example, presentation skills can be practised so that it is natural for you to present clearly and with confidence, make eye contact with your audience, and communicate ideas effectively.

The Cambridge Dictionary defines conditioning as: "the process of training or influencing a person or animal mentally so that they do or expect a particular thing without thinking about it."

What are the core habits you're conditioned with? And how would you like to improve them?

When I lamented that I was nervous to present to a senior leadership team, I remember one of my mentors stated: "Cindy, anxiety is a human event." I stomped away and concluded he showed little empathy, forgetting what it was like to be junior in his career. I felt dismissed.

When it came time to the presentation, I took a few deep breaths, looked at my audience and had this quick realisation. I thought despite my nerves if this is a natural human emotion, maybe what he was trying to tell me was that we all have anxiety. I did manage to get through the presentation, and in addition to feeling relieved that it was over, I knew presenting would continue to get easier.

Years later, I related this anecdote to my mentor, and he smiled and said: "I knew you were mad at me, my intent was for you to find the resolve to forge ahead." I thanked him and expressed my gratitude for creating that inner fortitude to move forward.

THE FLIPSIDE OF CONDITIONING

People often condition themselves unknowingly into taking up bad habits like smoking, drinking too much, overeating, or living a sedentary lifestyle. Having the skill to condition oneself knowingly requires a tremendous amount of self-control and is one of the most powerful habits a person can possess.

Conditioning isn't always fun either, so as a result, many people fail while trying. It takes at least 21 days to form a new habit - often longer. Maybe if you're finding yourself struggling to learn a specific new skill or habit, you can work on a more enjoyable one for the time being. When you strengthen your intentional conditioning habit itself, then it will become easier. Another alternative is to condition yourself in small increments, maybe one day per week for a period of at least 21 weeks.

ACTION STEPS FOR CONDITIONING

1. Think of a behaviour or skill that a colleague exhibits that you want to emulate but lack the confidence to try. Ask them for advice on how you can begin to work this into your repertoire.

2. Expect that it will be shaky or bumpy as you attempt your newly found skill.

3. Practice, practice, practice.

4. Take a video of yourself at regular intervals, critique yourself and monitor your progress.

Habit #18

MENTORING

"I know what mentoring can do, it can create careers, it can save lives."

~ Ervin László

They say teaching is one of the best ways of learning and retaining information. At the same time, it is also essential to have at least one person mentoring you. We often forget what it means to be junior in our career. Those days, if we are honest, harken back to insecurities, worries about doing the right thing, about pleasing our boss and about doing a good job. Along the way, hopefully we have all had mentors whether it was a formal mentor at work, a sports coach, a family member, or someone from our community. These relationships are invaluable and reciprocal.

As a mentor, you provide a confidential framework for that mentee to seek out your counsel. As you are not their manager, they can talk freely and get advice. How can they deal with someone on their team that is a naysayer? How can they enhance their brand or get help with presentation skills? And so many other leadership skills that mentors can help us with that are a benefit to our careers.

What is important in your role as a mentor is that you take away the mystique of your success. You can share that in fact that your road to success was not a straight line. You changed careers or changed directions several times. Plus, you made many mistakes.

As a mentor, this allows you to be human and vulnerable. You show your mentee you never did nor ever will have all the answers. Yet you were successful and perhaps even more successful because your path was varied. This takes the pressure off the mentee, permitting them to not have their career or the rest of their life figured out. Maybe it means many of us will have many careers across the course of our lives.

As a mentor, you can gain so much from the mentee. You are exposed to new and different ways of thinking. Your biases and ways of finding solutions are challenged. You emerge from the process a more well-rounded leader. Additionally, mentoring represents a great opportunity to enhance your own coaching skills as a leader.

When you choose to mentor, think about what skills you can offer. There is a great value when you can be specific around what expertise you want to share or impart. Are you a great public speaker? Are you known for your ability to problem solve? Do you excel at strategic thinking?

The same applies to your mentee. Make sure you ask them what specific skills they would like to work on. The greater both you and the mentee can base your relationship on specific skill acquisition, the more productive and fulfilling the engagement will be.

THE FLIPSIDE OF MENTORING

Set your mentee free. The mentor relationship runs the risk of creating a comfortable and safe place for the mentee. The goal of each mentor-mentee relationship should be time-limited and skill-based. You as a mentor want to encourage your mentee to be in charge and drive their own career. Provide them with the wings and confidence so they can soar.

ACTION STEPS FOR MENTORING

1. Identify the skills you would like to impart as a mentor.

2. Seek to learn from your mentee. This is a reciprocal relationship. They will broaden your thinking.

3. Have the mentee be specific about what skills they would like to acquire.

4. Make the engagement time-limited so your mentee can practice and grow.

Habit #19

GIVING

"No one is useless in this world who lightens the burdens of another."

~ Charles Dickens

Often people give, expecting a favour in return. A sort of social currency and transactional relationship. Although this form of leadership has worked for centuries, the context in which this chapter discusses giving is without expecting. It is vital to give and let the experience you get back be the receiver's experience of gratitude and happiness. When you give with no expectation of anything in return, your value set of compassion and sense of humanity rings true. You make a difference in people's lives and earn your respect as a leader who has the pulse on your team's well-being.

This generosity will strengthen your mastery and make you a go-to person at work and in life. Whether it be giving your time, energy, or wisdom, it can go a long way to brighten someone's day. After all, moods are virulent, and a happy team can make a difference towards achieving more extraordinary results.

Leaders who are giving do so in such a natural way. They are authentic and have the ability to put others first. They generally score high on emotional intelligence. For example, think about some of your favourite people within social groups. Bet there is a high probability that their giving trait is more advanced than the others in the same group. Giving certainly is one way to be liked. Our likeability quotient drives loyalty, followership and engagement. Simultaneously, it makes the giver feel good to be a stepping stone for achieving tangible results. We are proud of their achievements. We can watch with honour.

Here is a heartwarming story. One of my clients, a very successful business leader, decided she would like to give back and help those who are less fortunate. She determined that donating money to charitable institutions was not the way to go. She indicated that maybe her funds would improve, for example, patient surroundings such as enhancing a well-worn carpet or providing a fresh

106

coat of paint. Instead, she thought she could help out by watching out for human interest stories. In particular, those who suffered tragic events. So she set up a fund and when heartbreaking events occurred such as a family's house burning down, people being evicted because they could not pay their rent and many other personal crises she quickly and anonymously would send a significant amount of funds to help them. To this day, none of these families has a clue as to who their guardian angel was. What is exceptional is that this woman gave for the sheer compassion knowing she could make a difference. No plaques, no hospital wings, no shout outs to say, "hey, look at me."

Giving is the most benevolent habit of the lot and goes a long way in building your character over the longer term. It is also, by far, the most humble and historically mentioned trait in the world.

The Flipside of Giving

You don't have to be liked by everyone. Sometimes bullies may take advantage of givers, and giving in to their requests could perpetuate their antagonism. Giving is great, as long as you are assertive and know when to say "no" to suggestions when required. If you say "yes" to everything, then you run the risk of becoming a doormat.

For example, some employees always say yes to requests, particularly if coming from senior leaders. Although you may believe you are being helpful, you run the risk of being taken advantage of. Putting boundaries garners respect. If you don't, you may inadvertently do yourself an injustice. When it comes time for a promotion, decision-makers may worry about your capacity or tendency to be overextended.

Furthermore, the habits of giving and self-promoting balance each other out; however, as a word of caution; never boast about what you give to people. That is a sure-fire way to be viewed as self-serving.

ACTION STEPS FOR GIVING

1. Start your day with how you can extend yourself to others. Ask yourself what you value you can bring and make sure you stay authentic to yourself.

2. Put yourself in someone else's shoes and imagine their struggles.

3. Be selfless. In other words, think about how kind gestures can improve somebody else's life.

4. Give something away each day, even if it's simply a smile.

Habit #20

COMMUNICATING

"You never know when a moment and a few sincere words can have an impact on a life."

~ Zig Ziglar

One of the most important skills is to communicate effectively, whether it's conflict resolution, being assertive, asking for help, articulating clearly what you need, or the ability to form collegial relationships through respectful and transparent dialogue. There are many aspects of effective communication. Too many to cover here, but here are some of the highlights.

Communication is a complex art. To communicate effectively, you must consider your target audience. For example, if you speak to a group of actuaries versus technologists, you need to ensure the terms you use to describe your concepts are part of their lexicon. You also need to think in advance what the biases of the audience you are addressing include. Where might they push back, and what will resonate for them?

On a recent flight, a passenger sitting across the aisle from me appeared to become agitated suddenly. The person sitting next to him had just placed his bag into the overhead bin and pushed it to the very back. The agitated passenger started to scream and yell in a loud booming voice, "Do you know what you're doing? You're crushing my jacket. I have a very expensive suede jacket. It's worth thousands of dollars." The surrounding passengers became anxious at this outburst, as it was clear that this man had an explosive personality. Before we knew it, the flight attendant appeared on the scene. In a calming voice, she said, "Sir, may I be of help? Here is what I'm going to do. I am carefully and gently going to take your jacket, fold it, and you can watch me as I carefully place it neatly in the bin to ensure that your jacket is well preserved." She then asked, "Are you okay with this sir?" He then replied "I am." and appeared satisfied. Later on, during the flight, I remarked to the flight attendant on her savvy and elegance in diffusing a potentially volatile situation. She remarked, "Of course. I'm a mom."

This is such a great example of knowing how to use effective communication skills when dealing with difficult personalities.

Communication also entails accepting that if you explain something complex, although you might be passionate about the topic, others may be asking, "What's in it for me?" So you need to think about how this might better their universe. Why will they endorse your product or your path forward?

You also need to consider your tone of voice and body language. The goal is to be inclusive and respectful. Debate is healthy and encouraged, it does though, potentially lead to hurt feelings or attributions of not being a team player. Should this happen, you need to take ownership. If there is a conflict, then own the conflict. Being a mature leader means that it doesn't matter whose fault it is but rather apologise, explain that it wasn't your intent and that you want to start over.

The best communicators speak in short sound bites. They are concise and succinct. They do not get too granular; they allow the audience to ask questions or obtain more detail if need be. This allows you the communicator to not get lost in tangents and instead stay focused on the most salient aspects of what you would like to convey.

Your relationship network is your present and future currency. In other words, your technical skills are critical for you to complete your tasks and get your job done. Even if you don't have all the necessary skills, your organisation will provide you with the requisite training. As you advance within your company, what really matters even more than your technical skills is your relationship currency. What people say about you when you are not in the room really defines your personal brand. Your boss matters, but your boss is just one voice.

Active listening is one of the most important components of great communication. It means you are listening to see if the room gets you, are they confused, glazed over or sceptical? Listen closely for those cues and then learn to adapt to what you say to be more of a partner when communicating. By pausing, asking good questions, asking the audience for their views, this allows you to demonstrate you hear them and you are prepared to incorporate their feedback. After all, when you can do this, you are more likely to get buy-in and have everybody on board.

THE FLIPSIDE OF COMMUNICATION

A primary downside to communication is when you use communication to come across as having the best answer. Your job is to convey what you believe to be is the best approach but then step back and hear others out. If you charge ahead in isolation or the absence of new data and additional information, you will never bring others along. You will be perceived as a leader who tells people what to do rather than facilitate and coach others. Now, who would you rather work for?

As leaders, you also make a judgement call around what information to share. There are times when you only have partial information, and as much as you want to be transparent, you must wait until you have all the facts or truly understand the impact.

Furthermore, there are boundaries. There is certain information that is classified. You as a leader must decide what information gets shared with who and at what level. Always guide yourself by having an enterprise view.

If we all live long enough, we will have a manager or a peer who may be verbally abusive or unkind. When you are a junior in your career, you may feel grateful to have a job or not have the self-assuredness to push back. What is crucial to understand is that you and everyone on this planet deserve to be treated with respect. You will not be able to be productive and invest in your job if you are miserable. At the most basic level, every human interaction be it at work, at the grocery store or in your personal life must be characterised by respectful dialogue. If you are being treated in a way that is diminishing, then you need to speak up. If you don't, you condone that behaviour.

The first thing you must do is advise that person what they are doing and how it makes you feel. Hopefully, we can give them the benefit of the doubt, and they will apologise and modify how they communicate with you. Speaking up is showing courage and conviction.

The goal in your career is never to repress or push away feelings that make you uncomfortable. Speaking up can be hard to do; however, you can practice with a friend or trusted advisor. The bottom line is to be part of an organisation that provides the best environment to grow and practise these habits.

Action Steps for Communicating

1. Think of your target audience and tailor your message to that audience.

2. Ask yourself why you are communicating. What is your objective?

3. Ask your audience if they have any questions or concerns.

4. Listen to their feedback and incorporate what your team is saying, so you show you both care and are open to alternate ideas.

CONCLUSION

Mastery at work, like most business pursuits, requires ongoing commitment and practice. In embarking on this book, the goal was to provide you with the underpinning and philosophy for attaining effective habits. As you gain more exposure to the workplace, you will have time and possibilities to master your work.

Reading and keeping up to date with the latest in effective leadership styles and strategies to advance your career is vital. What is also paramount is the opportunity to practice and practice the skills outlined in this book.

Our intent is not to overwhelm you but rather to provide you with some very concrete strategies to create habit-forming behaviours. The great thing about mastery is that you can acquire these habits to become second nature.

When we get down or tired, we tend to say we don't have time; our lives are busy. However, it is like working out; most of us don't like the act of exercising. It can be painful, tedious and boring. However, when you make it a priority, you suddenly find the time. Then you reap the rewards. The goal is for you to develop a sense of efficacy, this then spurs you on to be motivated to be even more masterful.

The tips, skills and strategies imparted in this book are meant to be ones that are measurable and impactful. When you have achieved some of these habits, you will prosper not just in your work life but also in your personal life. Tremendous pride comes from the feeling of making a difference, impacting the world, improving the quality of life for those around you. Perhaps there is nothing more rewarding than bringing joy to others, and to the universe. When you have achieved this, you have truly mastered your workplace and your personal space.

ACKNOWLEDGEMENTS

First off, I would like to thank my co-producer, editor and colleague Derin Cag. Much to my delight, Derin reached out to me with the inspirational concept for this book, including the very practical framework that we all crave as managers and leaders. For everything in life, we all strive for, no matter what our journey is, we need help with the impetus and practical hands-on tips and strategies. Derin made it easy to establish a cadence of mutual respect and energy. He was incredibly instrumental in playing a multifaceted role of coach, mentor, and unwavering enthusiast. The outcome of this process is a book and practical guide that we believe offers valuable insights and lessons regarding how we can all create mastery and proficiency and success within our work lives. To this end, Derin kept me focused and helped me stay the course, and I am most proud of what we have created together.

My parents taught me the value of hard work, the need to strive and do your best in the spirit of kindness and integrity. They never told me to work hard; they never told me to be something in particular. Instead, they modelled hard work, left it open for me to find my path and were there when I stumbled and fell. Having my parents believe in me provided me with the determination to never quit, but rather to excel and forge ahead, respecting those around me.

Three men in my life deserve special mention: my life partner Leon, our son Josh, and our beloved and protective dog Ranger. Living with me is no easy feat. I have high standards, I am determined, and I can be relentless. There are times I am thankful for their laughter and their ability to tease me, a much-needed reality check on my need to slow down and enjoy where we are at the very moment. If it is possible to support my quest to experience life to the very fullest, they are always on my side and have been the best of friends and companions. And what can I say of our four-legged friend Ranger? He is extraordinarily devoted to the singular ambition in life to play fetch. If you are looking for an antidote for work-life balance, he is it!. He loves you no matter what and coming home each day being greeted with boundless love and energy can't be beaten.

I want to thank all my clients both organisationally and individually who have taught me about leadership over the years and what it truly means to be an effective and impactful leader. It is a privilege to lead others and for me as their coach, advisor and confident they have provided valuable on the job insights that have culminated in the best practices reflected in this book.

Made in the USA
Middletown, DE
21 March 2021

35256451R00068